Understanding Israel: A Christian View

by
Abbot Leo A. Rudloff, O.S.B.

I express the hope that my readers will notice that in analyzing the tragic struggle between Israel and the Arabs, I have tried to be fair to the Arab cause. At the same time, however, I do not want "even-handedness" to confuse the issue. It may be useful in this context to state at the beginning that I have no axe to grind. I am a gentile Christian. I lived in the city of Jerusalem for twenty years and have had extensive contacts with Arabs as well as Jews, in the beginning more with Arabs than with Jews.

It is clear that in any such conflict no party is completely without fault. But as in most or all such cases, there is one basic question underlying the conflict, and that question is not primarily the Palestinians. They are there and they pose a serious question which must be solved. But the Palestinian problem is itself the result of another question. And that question is simply and clearly: Has Israel a right to exist as a state, the majority of whose population is Jewish, and essentially as a homeland for the Jewish people? Although it grants freedom to all other persons living within its confines, it is fundamentally a Jewish state.

The Jewish People

It is one of the basic errors of Israel's enemies to overlook the fact that the Jews are a people. It is clearly stated in the Palestinian National Covenant adopted at a meeting of the Palestinian National Council in Cairo in July, 1968:

> "Judaism, in its character as a religion of revelation, is not a nationality, with an independent existence. Likewise the Jews are not one people with an independent personality." (Article 20).

But here lies a fundamental error. While Judaism is one of the world religions, the link between religion, people and land has always been one of the basic tenets of Jewish conviction. Jews are and always have been a people who have a right as any people to have their own political entity, their own country, and their own state. The fact that they have been deprived of that, due to external force, does not in the least alter that claim. Their struggle is, has been, and always will be a liberation movement if there ever was one.

This principle was stated in an excellent way in 1947 by Andrei Gromyko when he said:

> "It will be unjust if we ignore the aspiration (of the Jews to create their own state) and deny the Jewish people the right to realize it." And when the Arab states attacked Israel in 1948, in a speech on May 21, 1948 the same Andrei Gromyko characterized that action as "aimed at the suppression of a national movement."

Later we will see how the Jews have maintained their claim to the land and to peoplehood through the centuries. The denial of this claim is at the basis of the tragic conflict. Suffice it to quote a few statements of Arab leaders from recent times:

> "God has gathered the Zionists together from the corners of the world so that the Arabs can kill them all at one stroke. This was impossible before, owing to their dispersion." (Ibrahim Tahwy, Assistant Secretary of the Liberation Rally, in the Cairo daily *Al-Ahram* of September 6, 1956).

On May 26, 1967, after Nasser had concentrated troops in

the Sinai Peninsula and closed the Straits of Tiran to Israel shipping, he said:

> "I know that by concentrating troops and by blockading Israel I invite war. I am ready for it. The end will be Israel's destruction."

On June 1, 1967, President Abdul Mohammed Araf of Iraq said:

> "The existence of Israel is a mistake that must be rectified . . . Our goal is clear — to wipe Israel off the map."

But I will not tire my reader with an unmanageable list of such statements, even though I could quote many more. Here is only one recent addition.

A Democratic Palestinian State?

In March, 1970 a symposium was held at the invitation of the editorial board of the Lebanese newspaper *El-Anwar* on the idea of the creation of a democratic Palestinian state. Among the participants were representatives of the Palestine Liberation Movement (Al Fatah), the Arab Liberation Front, the Popular Front for the Liberation of Palestine, and two other groups. While there were many differences of opinion, there was agreement on one matter, which was expressed by one of the representatives present:

> "The State can only be created on the ruins of the Zionist entity and the destruction of the State of Israel." (Proceedings published in the weekly magazine of *El-Anwar* on March 8 and 15, 1970).

In the meantime, the PLO has amply demonstrated that it has wrought havoc in the democratic state of Lebanon. The Lebanese people have finally revolted against the dictatorial domination of a foreign body in their midst, but Lebanon is also bleeding to death. According to the Vatican Radio, the key factor in the Lebanese conflict is the presence in Lebanon of Palestinian refugees who formed "something similar to a state within the Lebanese state." (Religious News Service, July 28, 1976).

All the talk about a "democratic Palestinian state" is a slogan adopted for propaganda purposes, because it "met with remarkable world response." (Minutes from the Congress of July, 1968).

It all flows from the basic error denying peoplehood to the Jews, as mentioned above.

Developments in Lebanon and their aftermath have to be watched. At the present moment, the PLO is a weakened force which bungled in Lebanon, in Entebbe and elsewhere, but has again and again amply demonstrated that it is given to violence, ruthless murder, and terror without any regard to the lives or safety of civilians and peaceful travelers. The PLO seems to be in trouble elsewhere, too, e.g. in Kuwait. (cf. *New York Times*, September 1, 1976). It looks at present as if it is not only falling apart but is being recognized more and more as a group of outlaws.

The Very Existence of Israel

It is not a question of boundaries, then, nor of refugees, nor of the rights of the Palestinians, but of the very existence of Israel. In a speech delivered in Mecca before an audience of Moslem pilgrims and diplomats on December 30, 1973, King Faisal of Saudi Arabia said (as reported by the Saudi Press Agency):

> "It is unfortunate that some people are trying to promote the so-called historical rights of the Jews in Jerusalem. The Jews have no Holy Places in Jerusalem. The so-called Temple of Solomon was carried away by the Romans when they conquered Palestine. Thus the Jews have no connection with the Holy City, they have no rights of presence in the city, or rule there, and their feet should not tread within it . . .
>
> "The Jews deviated from the Law of Moses and tried to murder Jesus Christ because they did not want the Laws of God to be observed . . .
>
> "They are the enemies of Islam and it is specifically stressed in the Koran that the Jews are the worst sworn enemies of the Moslems . . .
>
> "We shall mobilize all our forces and resources to redeem our Holy Places and liberate Jerusalem from the Zionists and Communists . . . which are both the most dangerous enemies of Allah and the faith of Islam.
>
> "If there is no Jewish connection with Jerusalem, what

possible connection can there be with the rest of the country? But even if they had some kind of claim, it is forfeit by virtue of their enmity to Islam and their attempted deicide."

This statement of King Faisal also testifies to the widespread anti-Semitism rampant in Arab lands. This is further documented by innumerable texts distributed to students and soldiers, reminiscent of the worst caricatures of the Nazi period. The well-known journalist Amin Mansour wrote in the representative daily *Al-Akhbar* of August 19, 1973:

> "History has begun to vindicate the anti-Semitic policy of Hitler. The world now understands that Hitler was right and that there was a logical reason for constructing the cremation furnaces in order to punish those who show such scorn for the principles of humanity."

King Faisal also made the following statement in an interview with Arnauld de Borchgrave of *Newsweek*, as published December 21, 1970:

> "Zionism and communism are working hand in glove to block any settlement to restore peace . . . It's all part of a great plot, a grand conspiracy. Communism is a Zionist creation designed to fulfill the aims of Zionism."

It was in Arab countries that Hitler's *Mein Kampf* was translated and published in Arabic. The infamous *Protocols of the Elders of Zion*, recognized everywhere else as a forgery, was also published in many Arabic editions (a so-called luxury edition appeared in Beirut in 1967).

This way the stage was set for the United Nations resolution of November 10, 1975, calling Zionism a form of racism, a resolution which U.S. Ambassador Daniel Patrick Moynihan called infamous. He also quoted the term "obscene" which the U.S. Representative to the Social, Humanitarian, and Cultural Committee, Leonard Garment, had used in a similar context three weeks earlier. Moynihan also correctly said:

> "The abomination of anti-Semitism . . . has been given the appearance of international sanction."

Church authorities of almost all denominations have also

come out strongly in condemnation of that outrageous United Nations resolution.

Are there any signs of a change — if not of heart, then at least of approach — among the Arabs in recent years? There might be some. President Sadat of Egypt has at least entered negotiations with great and admirable courage. He may be resigned to a co-existence with an independent Israel. Some observers think there might be even some signs of readiness to compromise inside the PLO, despite the unyielding rhetoric. (cf. an editorial in the *New York Times* of August 16, 1976) a new generation of Palestinian leaders may also have emerged on the West Bank and in Gaza who might be ready to live in peace with Israel.

We shall speak a little later specifically about the question of the Palestinians. But so far, no responsible Arab statesman has clearly and officially repudiated the three Nos — "No peace, no negotiation, no recognition" — to which "kings and presidents agreed" in the famous formula of Khartoum of August 1967.

Early Arab Friendship

Did Arabs always take an implacable stance towards Jewish resettlement in Palestine? If we review history, we will find that after World War I Arab leaders were entirely friendly to the Zionist movement. King Hussein of the Hejaz (now Saudi Arabia) wrote at that time:

> "We saw the Jews . . . streaming to Palestine from Russia, Germany, Austria, Spain, America. . . . The cause of causes could not escape those who had the gift of deeper insight; they knew that the country was for its original sons, for all their differences, a sacred and beloved homeland . . . The return of these exiles to their homeland will prove materially and spiritually an experimental school for their brethren." (*Al Qigla*, Mecca, No. 183, March 23, 1918; quoted in George Antonius, "The Arab Awakening," p. 269).

Hussein's son, the Emir Faisal, who later became King of Iraq, wrote in his famous letter of March 3, 1919, to Felix Frankfurter at the time of the Paris Peace Conference after World War I:

"We feel that Arabs and Jews are cousins in race, having suffered similar oppression at the hands of powers stronger than themselves, and by a happy coincidence have been able to take the first steps toward the attainment of their national ideals together.

"We Arabs, especially the educated among us, look with the deepest sympathy on the Zionist movement. Our deputation here in Paris is fully acquainted with the proposals submitted yesterday by the Zionist Organization to the Peace Conference. We will do our best . . . to help them through; we will wish the Jews a most hearty welcome home."

Emir Faisal was the Chief Arab delegate to the Paris Peace Conference. On January 3, 1919, he concluded an agreement with Dr. Chaim Weizmann, endorsing the Balfour Declaration and recognizing Palestine as a separate Jewish entity, with which the Arab State would maintain diplomatic relations. There was, however, a reservation attached to Faisal's agreement, and here we come to the reason why he later repudiated that agreement and turned anti-Zionist. The reservation was that Britain and France must meet Arab demands in other territories.

The Estrangement

Faisal and other Arab leaders felt they had been betrayed by the British, who had promised Faisal a Damascus-based Kingdom of Greater Syria, and his brother, Abdullah, a kingdom in Iraq. At the same time, however, or so it seemed to the Arab leaders, the British had concluded an agreement with France, creating spheres of influence in a way that gave France control of Syria and Lebanon. The French did not want an Arab king in Damascus. Faisal finally was made King of Iraq, and to satisfy Abdullah, the kingdom of Transjordan was carved out of Palestine.

Clearly, the anti-Zionist attitude developed only by extension. It was really anti-British. This was a tragic development, for which the Jews cannot be held responsible. Undoubtedly that era was Colonialist and Imperialist, but to equate the Jewish resettlement of Palestine with such forces is utterly unjust.

The Grand Mufti

There is still another source of Arab antagonism, and that source was much more vicious. The man who constantly instigated anti-Jewish riots and fostered hatred of the Jews, a person whom I do not hesitate to characterize as sinister, is the former Mufti of Jerusalem, appointed Grand Mufti of Palestine by the British: Haj Amin al-Husseini.

During World War II, the Grand Mufti fled to Iraq, and there he started a lively correspondence with Nazi officials in Germany. Expressing warmest sympathies for the Nazis, the Mufti was rewarded with a personal reply from Hitler, who wrote: "Germans and Arabs have common enemies in the English and in the Jews, and are united in the struggle against them."

When the Iraqi revolt against the British broke down, al-Husseini went to Berlin, where he was photographed in intimate conversation with Hitler, Himmler and SS generals. According to depositions at the Nuremberg trials, the Mufti was largely responsible for the "liquidation" of Jews, especially in Bosnia. According to Robert M. W. Kempner, the former deputy prosecutor at the Nuremberg trials, the Mufti received 90,000 marks per month from Hitler (Das Dritte Reich im Kreuzverhör, p. 277f).

After the collapse of the Nazi regime in Germany, al-Husseini went to Egypt. He attracted top Nazis to Egypt such as Franz Rademacher, General Dirlewanger and Johann von Leers. Many of them hid behind Arabic names: Von Leers, for example, was known in Cairo as Omar Amin. He was political adviser to the Information Department, appointed on recommendation of the Mufti. Von Leers died in 1965.

The Arab Israelis

The Arab estrangement and the effect of Nazi propaganda is utterly tragic, especially since it poisons the very roots of relations between Israelis and Arabs, both the Arabs outside of Israel and the Arab Israelis within Israel. The surrounding Arabs try to use the Arab Israelis and those in the Israel-controlled territories as a fifth column, which puts them under a cloud. I do not intend to defend every single action of the Israeli Government in regard to the Arab Israelis. I am uneasy, particularly, over the treatment of the Arabs of the two loyal villages of Biram and Ikrit in Upper Galilee.* But it is very difficult for one not completely informed on the security situation to pass a decisive judgment on these matters. Only after peace is restored between Arabs and Israelis can these questions be resolved to the satisfaction of all parties involved, meeting to negotiate on an equal basis.

The status of the Arab minority in Israel, both Moslem and Christian, is also of genuine concern to the Israelis. There was a revealing dialogue published in *The Christian Century*, February 4, 1970, p. 139-141, between the Greek-Catholic (Arab) Archbishop of Galilee, Monsignor Joseph Raya, who often also spoke for Moslem Arabs, and Professor Zvi Werblowsky of the Hebrew University. I am happy to call both of these gentlemen my friends. Archbishop Raya always speaks clearly for loyalty to the State of Israel, although he often criticizes individual actions of the government.** In the above-mentioned dialogue, Professor Werblowsky says:

"The relationship to our non-Jewish population within Israel and to our Arab neighbors . . . creates immense social, political and moral problems. The Zionist achievement, for all its being in the profoundest historical sense a manifestation of historic justice for the Jewish people, somehow involves an injustice to others . . . No (human) activity is perfectly righteous and just. In whatever one does, there is an element . . . of sin. Now it is possible, of course, to take a very simplistic look at Israel and regard it as unmitigated evil, the very incarnation of brutal injustice. The Arab leaders surrounding us take such a view. But for us Jews it is an existentially tragic struggle between two kinds of justice, if I may use that phrase. It is the necessity of realizing that which we think to be the maximum of justifiable justice and combining with it a minimum of unavoidable injustice. It is precisely here

---

*Some of the villagers are personally known to me. Some are employed on the Benedictine Farm in Galilee and live on church property.

**It was over the question of loyalty to the State of Israel, which he staunchly defended in connection with the Capudji affair, that Archbishop Raya resigned his position recently.

that we have to find a working formula. What this means is more than consideration of the basic human aspirations of our Arab minority. It is not enough for us to say, 'All right, we Jews in Israel can be decent to Arabs here.' Much more is needed. For these people have cultural and spiritual aspirations, not only rights as citizens. They have talents and qualities as people who belong to a long and rich cultural heritage in the Arab world . . . Keep in mind that Zionist Israel is a very young country. It was born of a tragedy of unparalleled magnitude: the Holocaust. It was brought into being by a major upsurge of nationalism. Such events do not provide the atmosphere for genuine pluralism in a new society. As we manage to survive and get past the present climactic moment, we must then proceed to authentic pluralistic life in Israel."

Much Has Been Achieved

It must also be stated that much has already been achieved in that respect. Not only can an Arab cabinet member like Abdul-Aziz Zouabi, Deputy Minister of Health in Israel, say to an audience of 2500 American Jewish women on August 23, 1971, that there is "no intrinsic opposition between my Israeli citizenship and my Arab patriotism" (*The New York Times*, August 24, 1971); but an Arab journalist and literary editor of the Arab newspaper *El Anba*, published in Jerusalem, Mahmoud Abassi, could say in an interview (in Brookline, Massachusetts) among other things:

"I have found a lot of misunderstanding among well-meaning people of all shades. Some think the Arabs in Israel live under military government and suffer a lot, have no representation in Parliament, that we have lost our culture, that we are very poor and don't have the opportunity to work. It is not true."

He admits that the Arab Israelis have not yet arrived at the ideal situation, although they have achieved considerable improvement in all facets of life. (cf. *Boston Sunday Globe*, April 5, 1970, p. 37).

Do the Arabs, living in Palestine, i.e. in Israel and the occupied territories, look to the PLO as their spokesmen and representatives? Perhaps at present they do, in want of better representation. But it seems to be apparent also that many among them would prefer a more moderate representation and would be ready to come to terms with the existing and viable Jewish State of Israel.

A Moral Right to Exist

Let us examine the questions of Israel's moral and juridical right to exist. If we look at the land which had been Palestine between the end of the Second Commonwealth in the year 70, when the Temple in Jerusalem was destroyed by the Romans, and the establishment of the State of Israel in the year 1948, there are two striking features for anyone to see who dispassionately considers the history of the land.

The first is the continuous presence of the Jews in the land, without their merging into any of the racial and religious communities which held sway there. There were continuous revolts against the Roman conquerors. True, they were finally crushed by the violence of superior force (not without the heroic sacrifice of Masada), but the people clung tenaciously to the land, which remained the center of Jewish life. The Mishna and the Palestinian Talmud developed there. A large Jewish community survived in Galilee, where, for example, the old synagogue in the village of Pekiin, in the lovely Galilean hills, still bears witness to continuous Jewish existence, all the way back to biblical times. There were Jewish communities in parts of the coastal plain and in Judaea. There existed a fairly substantial agricultural Jewish population, especially in Galilee, at the time of the Crusades. There were important Jewish communities in Jerusalem, Acco, Haifa, Jaffa, Ashkelon, Tiberias, Ramleh and Gaza. After the expulsion of the Jews from Spain in 1492 there arose the spiritual center in Safad where the Shulchan Aruch, the code of law, was produced, together with other works of mysticism. In the sixteenth century, Tiberias became a great Jewish center.

Other Civilizations

On the other hand, and that is the second striking feature, all attempts to establish other civilizations in the land ended in failure. Edward H. Flannery summarizes the history of

Palestine in the following manner:

"A crossroad between Asia, Europe and Africa, Palestine has remained (from the destruction of Jerusalem until today) the neglected province of absent rulers and the runway of fluctuating populations. First a Roman province, then Byzantine, it came under Arab rule in 637 A.D. The Arabs ruled it as foreign conquerors for 400 years to lose it in 1071 to the Seljuk Turks (1071-1099). Christian Crusaders occupied it for nearly two centuries, after which it was ruled by Tartars, Mongols (1244-1260), Mamelukes of Egypt (1260-1517), and Ottoman Turks, who held it until it was mandated by the Allies to Great Britain at the close of World War I. Thus it remained an amorphous geopolitical entity without clear boundaries, a thankless host to Jews, Arabs, Christian pilgrims, Bedouin, and the various agents of its conquerors. In the last thirteen centuries, it has changed hands fourteen times and has at no time been an independent country. No national claim to it was made by any group within it." ("Foundations of the State of Israel," in: *The Lamp*, June 1969, p. 5f).

For none of those powers was it a beloved and cared-for homeland. It is as if the land did not respond. That is, in fact, the traditional rabbinic interpretation of Lev.26:32: "I will make such a desolation of the land, that your enemies who come to live there will be appalled by it [or according to another translation: will be desolate, too]." (cf. R. J. Zwi Werblowsky, "Israel et Eretz Israel," in: *Les Temps Modernes*, 1967, n.253 bis, p. 384).

Resettlement in the Modern Period

The Jewish people have never ceased to assert its bond to the land of Israel. Israel and Jerusalem were ever in the memory and in the yearning of the Jewish people. In the daily services Jews say: "Blessed are You, Lord who builds Jerusalem." No meal was ever concluded without saying: "Build Jerusalem, speedily, in our days." No Passover Seder, no Day of Atonement (Yom Kippur) was ever celebrated without saying: "Next year in Jerusalem." There is no such attachment to any land anywhere else in the world like the attachment of the Jewish people to the land of Israel. "The merit of living in the land of Israel equals the merit of observing all the commandments of the Torah" is the traditional formulation of Jewish sentiment towards the Holy Land.

Jewish immigration to Palestine in modern times began in the late nineteenth century. In 1850 there were 20,000 Jews in Palestine; in 1914 there were about 100,000. They lived on land that was legally purchased from Arab — often absentee — owners, and for which they often paid exorbitant prices. The Jews bought it dunam by dunam, and not a single Arab was displaced.* On the contrary, the Arab population doubled in that same period. They were attracted by the economic progress being made. The years for which we have reliable statistics are 1922-1931. In those years, about 94,000 Jews immigrated, and approximately 60,000 Arabs. In other words, the Arab immigration of that period accounted for 36.8 percent of total immigration. The number of Jewish-owned enterprises increased from 1,850 to 6,007, and 60 percent of the industrial work force it employed in 1927 was Arab. (cf. Fred M. Gottheil, "Arab Immigration into Pre-State Israel: 1922-1931," in: Middle East Information Series, XXIV, Fall 1973, p. 13-22). Prior to 1922 Arabs were leaving the country; after 1922 they began to come in — from Syria, Iraq, Lebanon, Transjordan and Egypt. The figures for Jerusalem are even more impressive. The Encyclopedia Britannica of 1911 gives the following figures for 1905, reporting the Turkish census: of a total population of about 60,000, there were 7,000 Moslems, 13,000 Christians and 40,000 Jews.

With regard to land ownership, British government statistics show that in May, 1948 when the State of Israel was established, 8.6 percent of the land was owned by Jews and 3.35 percent by Arab Israelis, while 16.9 percent had been abandoned by Arab owners who fled the country. More than 70 percent of the land was vested in the Mandatory Power and so reverted to Israel as its legal heir.

The period of the British Mandate saw an increase of the

---

*The Peel Commission reported 664 acceptable Arab claims for resettlement, and 347 of these accepted government resettlement. The remainder refused, either because they had found satisfactory employment elsewhere or because they were not accustomed to irrigated cultivation or the climate of the new areas (Peel Commission Report, Chap. 9, para, 60).

Jewish population of Palestine to almost three-quarters of a million, with a correspondingly great increase in the numbers and prosperity of the Arab population. There was also a substantial illegal Arab immigration, even after Great Britain had severely restricted Jewish immigration. The Jews constituted approximately one-third of the total population, and the United Nations Partition Plan (of which more in the next section) tried to find an equitable solution to the conflicting claims of the inhabitants by allotting those parts of Palestine to the Jewish "homeland," in which there was a majority of Jews, the balance to become another Arab state.

A Legal Right to Exist

And so we come to the events of recent history, and to a demonstration of Israel's legal right to exist.

The story is too well known to be repeated here in detail. Reference must be made, however, to the main events. The Balfour Declaration was issued on November 2, 1917. True, the Declaration in itself was not a legal document, but it was accepted by the world community *including the Arabs*, as mentioned previously, and provided the rationale for the San Remo Conference of April 1920 and the League of Nations decision of July 24, 1922 (Art. 4) in which Great Britain was charged "to secure the cooperation of all Jews who are willing to assist in the establishment of a Jewish National Home in Palestine." The interpretation of "National Home" as a state was accepted by the various political authorities. Emir Faisal, in his January 1919 written agreement with Weizmann, stipulated a Palestine, separated from the "Arab State" by boundaries to be worked out later, and "duly accredited" Jewish and Arab agents who would maintain diplomatic relations.

In its preamble the Mandate speaks of "reconstituting their (the Jews') national home in that country." The United Nations Special Committee on Palestine (UNSCOP) found that they could not divorce the question of a Jewish commonwealth from the fate of the dispossessed Jews of Europe. Nor could they bypass the historic claims of the Jewish people, especially when placed against the millions of square miles of territorial grants that the Arabs had received after World War I. They came to the further conclusion that neither a federated nor a bi-national state was any longer possible. The only solution was partition.

Thus the partition plan of 1947 was worked out, in which those parts of the country in which the Jews formed the majority were allotted to the Jewish State, while the rest was destined for the Arabs. The latter, unfortunately had no designated authority *within* Palestine to speak for them. A tragic solution was forced on them from outside, by the *Arab* powers.

A Jewish State

On November 29, 1947, by more than the required two-thirds majority vote, the General Assembly of the United Nations, the recognized power responsible for mandates, adopted the Partition Plan. In its resolution the General Assembly affirmed the creation of "a Jewish State." It recommended

> ". . . to all members of the United Nations, the adoption and implementation, with regard to the future Government of Palestine, of the Plan of Partition with Economic Union . . .; Calls upon the inhabitants of Palestine to take such steps as may be necessary on their part to put this plan into effect; Appeals to all Governments and all peoples to refrain from taking any action which might hamper or delay the carrying out of these recommendations . . ."

On May 14, 1948 the State of Israel was proclaimed, effective as of the expiration of the British Mandate, just past midnight. Ten minutes after its official birth, Israel was recognized by the United States, followed almost immediately by Guatemala and thereafter by the Soviet Union and most Western powers. On May 11, 1949, by vote of the General Assembly, Israel became a member of the United Nations.

However, on the very day the British withdrew and the State of Israel was proclaimed, the armies of Egypt, Transjordan, Syria, Lebanon and Iraq marched against Israel and thus became the aggressors against the legitimately established State of Israel. The partition lines were obliterated, and the Palestinian Arab State disappeared, annexed by Transjordan. And the refugee problem was born.

Arab Refugees

Everybody feels sympathetic to the Arab refugees.* A solution must be found. Israel has often expressed its readiness to help towards such a solution, but not at the jeopardy of its own existence. Israel does not want to commit suicide. Statements like the following help shape the reactions and thinking of every Israeli:

> "In demanding the restoration of the refugees to Palestine, the Arabs intend that they shall return as the masters of the homeland and not as slaves. More explicitly, they intend to annihilate the State of Israel." (Dr. Mohammed Salah ed-Din, Egyptian Minister of Foreign Affairs in *Al Misr*, October 11, 1949).
>
> "If the Arabs return to Israel, Israel will cease to exist." (President Nasser to the *"Zuercher Woche,"* September 1, 1961).
>
> "The day of the realization of the Arab hope for the return of the refugees to Palestine means the liquidation of Israel." (Abdulla al-Yafi, Prime Minister of Lebanon, in the Lebanese Parliament, as reported in *Al Hayat*, Lebanon, April 29, 1966).

Responsibility for the refugee problem does not rest principally on Israel. There is no doubt that the first refugees left of their own accord. There is a controversy, however, as to whether *formal* orders were issued by Arab authorities for them to leave. According to the *Bulletin of the Research Group for European Migration Problems*, The Hague, January-March 1957 (pp. 10f):

> "As early as the first months of 1948, the Arab League issued orders exhorting the people to seek temporary refuge in the neighboring countries, later to return to their abodes in the wake of the victorious Arab armies and obtain their share of abandoned Jewish property."

---

*The number of Arab refugees has always been vastly inflated by propagandists. According to a statement by UNRWA in 1952, all births were eagerly announced and deaths, wherever possible, passed over in silence, so that the family could continue to collect rations for the deceased. Henri Labousse, UNRWA director, told a Palestinian refugee conference in Jerusalem, on July 20, 1955: "There are refugees who hold as many as 500 UNRWA ration cards."

A Memorandum to Members

On April 27, 1948 the Arab National Committee, refusing to sign a truce, sent the following "memorandum" to the Arab League member governments:

"When the delegation entered the conference room it proudly refused to sign the truce and asked that the evacuation of the Arab population and their transfer to neighboring Arab countries be facilitated . . . The military and civil authorities and the Jewish representatives expressed their profound regret. The mayor of Haifa (Mr. Shabtai Levi) adjourned the meeting with a passionate appeal to the Arab population to reconsider its decision." ("Refugees in the Middle East," N.Y., 1967, p. 15)

Mahmoud Seif ed-Din Irani, a refugee from Jaffa, wrote (in his book, "With the People," Amman, 1956): "We left the country of our own free will believing we were on a short visit."

Nimr al-Hawari, former commander of the paramilitary Arab Youth Organization in Palestine, says (in his book "The Secret Behind the Disaster"): "The Arabs were confused by promises and deluded by their leaders."

The Jordanian daily, *Ad-Difaa*, reported on September 6, 1954: "The Arab Governments told us: 'Get out so that we can get in' — so we got out, but they did not get in."

The British police in Haifa reported to headquarters in Jerusalem on April 26, 1948: "Every effort is being made by the Jews to persuade the Arab population to stay and carry on with their normal lives, to get their shops and businesses open and to be assured that their lives and interests will be safe."

Population Exchange

It can also be argued that with more than half a million, perhaps as many as 800,000, Jewish refugees coming to Israel *from Arab countries* (besides the millions from other countries), there has been an unplanned population exchange. I would not have recommended such an exchange, but exchanges have been carried out in other areas of conflict. At any rate, the Jewish refugees from Arab countries should not be forgotten. I have seen the miserable condition of those refugees in their immigration camps, as I have seen Arab refugee camps. The difference between them is that the Jews were fully absorbed in the life of Israel, while the Arabs themselves kept the Arab refugees as pawns in the political chess games of the Arab governments.

A Distorted Case

It has often been argued that the Arab refugees fled in panic after Jewish "atrocities," and the case of the village of Deir Yassin is adduced constantly in that context. That it is brought up again and again has always appeared to me tacit testimony in favor of Israel: It seems to be the only case available. Deir Yassin is not a glorious page in the history of the war of 1947/48. However, it is vastly distorted by the Arabs. It *was* a war action. Deir Yassin, together with Castel, was an obstacle on the road to Jerusalem, where 150,000 Jewish civilians were under siege, fighting for their lives, for their supply of food and water. Deir Yassin sheltered one company of Iraqi troops and another company of Palestinian Arab soldiers. The inhabitants of Deir Yassin were warned by loudspeakers of the impending attack. Some two hundred villagers took advantage of the warning and were brought out to safety. Without going into the details of that sad story, I quote the testimony of an Arab survivor, an inhabitant of Deir Yassin. Yunes Ahmed Assad wrote in the Jordanian daily *Al Urdun* of April 9, 1955:

> "The Jews never intended to hurt the population of the village, but were forced to do so after they met enemy fire from the population, which killed the Irgun commander."

The only inaccuracy in this statement is the report on the Irgun commander's death; actually he was wounded. Evidently, Assad saw him fall and drew the wrong conclusion. The villagers had used a ruse, showing white surrender flags and then shooting at the Irgun troops.

But more than three months before Deir Yassin, on December 30, the Arabs massacred 41 unarmed Jewish workers at the Haifa oil refineries; one week after Deir Yassin, they ambushed a convoy carrying Jewish doctors and nurses to the Hadassah Hospital on Mt. Scopus and set fire to the buses, killing 77 men and women as they sought to escape the flames. Nor were these massacres unique. There had been widespread attacks on unarmed Jews in Jerusalem and other places as far back as 1921, and eight years later, in 1929, similar massacres of Jews in Motza, Safed and Hebron — where the Jews were utterly defenseless — as well as attacks on Jews in Jerusalem and Tel Aviv and villages all over the country.

I recall these events not to irritate old wounds — it would be better to be able to transcend these horrors. But they must not be used to foment hatred and aggression.

Once the war had started, some Arab villages where troops found resistance were razed and the inhabitants driven out. But the numerous Arab villages in the Galilee today testify to the fact that there was no general policy of expulsion.

The Palestinian Question

Talking about the refugees does not exhaust the entire question of the Palestinians. In fact, the Palestinians refuse to be classified as refugees. Many of them are refugees, but many others are not. They claim nationality and peoplehood as Palestinians, and consider their struggle as a liberation movement.

It would be beyond the scope of this booklet to give an adequate response to the very complicated and involved questions of a Palestinian state. This pamphlet is intended only to offer a few points to be considered.

The present writer has had ample opportunity to see the hurt and to empathize with the many Arabs who suffered from being, as they put it "strangers in the country of our birth." As we have already indicated, the whole problem needs further consideration.

But first of all: Palestine has never been a political entity, as we have pointed out.

Then, the U.N. partition plan had envisaged an independent Arab state in Palestine, along with the Jewish state. Unfortunately, the Arabs refused, while the Jews accepted.

Further, a Palestinian state on PLO terms would mean the

destruction of Israel. The PLO proposed a secular state in which Jews who were living in Palestine before the "Zionist invasion" would reside. Jews would be a definite minority. And Jews know what living in any country as a minority means.

Jews have always lived as a suppressed minority in Arab countries (as they have also lived in other countries, to be sure). They were definitely second-class citizens. (Still, in April 1972 Egyptian President Sadat cited the expulsion of Jews by Mohammed as justification for not negotiating with Israel:

> "The most splendid thing our prophet Mohammed did was to evict the Jews from the Arabian peninsula. We know their history with our prophet. They are a mean and treacherous people.")

Further, it is difficult to say whether a mini-state on the West Bank and in Gaza would be viable. It could easily become a tool in the hands of other, greater powers and thus become a great danger for Israel.

Actually, the country where most Palestinians live and have always lived is the present kingdom of Jordan. There already is a Palestinian state.

But I intend only to state these points for consideration. It is beyond the purpose of this booklet to propose a solution to this problem. The aim of this pamphlet is to emphasize Israel's right to exist.

Effective Guarantees

One last word is necessary to understand Israel's position in the present situation and its reluctance to give up conquered territory without effective guarantees. Israelis remember all too well what happened after the Sinai campaign of 1956. They withdrew from the Suez Canal and all territory conquered at that time. They trusted the paper guarantees they were given. A United Nations force was stationed in Sinai and at Sharm el-Sheikh. Just one word from Nasser and the UN personnel were removed and the war of 1967 started. At that time British Foreign Secretary George Brown stated (on May 18, 1967, at a dinner of the United Nations Association in London):